# YOUR TWENTIES
## GO SOMETHING LIKE . . .

# Your Twenties
GO SOMETHING LIKE . . .

## CLIFF PEREZ

New Universe Press | San Diego

Copyright © 2018 by Cliff Perez
Copyright © 2018 by New Universe Press

All rights reserved. This book or any portion thereof may not be reproduced or used in any manner whatsoever without the express written permission of the publisher except for the use of brief quotations in a book review.

Printed in the United States of America

First printing, 2018

ISBN 978-0-9994343-0-7

www.NewUniversePress.com

*This book is dedicated to you...*

# Contents

## PART ONE

Your 20's Go Something Like . . . *3*

Giggles *4*

Empty Tea Party *5*

Millennial *6*

The White Rabbit *7*

Craft *8*

A.I. *9*

Cliché 'Merica *11*

Black Cat *13*

Dead Babies *14*

Night Terror *15*

Oliver Twist *16*

People-Controlled Content *18*

Pop Control *19*

Selfie *20*

Tiptoe *21*

Two Lines and Freebird *22*

## PART TWO

Love *25*

Vines *27*

Teen Mom OG *28*

Messiah *29*

The Lotto *30*

Changes  *31*
White Girl  *32*
Mania  *33*
Mad Men  *34*
Forgot My Lines  *35*
Forever Young  *36*
New School  *37*

**A MESSAGE FROM THE WRITER**
Final Essay  *41*

**EPILOGUE**
The Mirror Is Me  *45*
Girls Are Just Boys with Makeup  *46*
Old Ladies Write Poetry  *47*
Rashad  *48*
Send in the Clowns  *49*
Self Portrait of a Young Artist by Not James Joyce  *51*

# PART ONE

## Your 20's Go Something Like . . .

. . . an explosion
in a midnight sky
swinging swirls
of rushing air
on my smile,
An inherent
Newtonian pull
grabbing at
ambitions from
my bowels
wallowing
in unresolved
mystery problems,
The uneven bars,
Unbalanced,
And made one way.

Mushroom clouds famously
fading into
the next phase,

Then you realize
that all you never
wanted is yours . . .

. . . then you like it.

**Giggles**

Humid dew
on pedals
swerving in
and out
of congested
traffic,
Drifting towards
black holes
or halves
of candy sticks
on dare bets for
keeps,
Wrestling matches
scheduled
for the Main
Event . . .
Sunsets
on the rooftops
of floating trees,
The giggles flickering
around in your ears.

**Empty Tea Party**

Empty beer cans
softly placed on
a vagrant
concrete ledge
to a tune
of courtesies
and soft
smell gestures
penetrating the
ghastliest
ghostly notions
of pompous
people laughing
at the
homeless man
who doesn't
realize that
nobody
is there.

**Millennial**

Good help
hard to find
in futuristic days,
You keep smelling right
through my
aforementioned
selves,
A Gemini revolver;
Dueling impersonality.

## The White Rabbit

Opaque cracks
of earth running
from the fog of bore,
So forward,
And you could
hear small steps of
pitter patter from
miles
away rippling through
vast desolate
waves of sound,
Manic in posture,
Spiraling
through the soft
bristles of
sleepy sunshine.

Hearts racing to
tea tasting like
unflavored water,
No thyme.

I keep chasing
wholes
in half the
time
as everyone else,
But I'm late . . .

**Craft**

*Hey, you should try our super pretentious IPA.*

"Is it special?"

*Oh ya — we fill it with all the finest adjectives, lace it with alcohol, and tell you that you're a connoisseur.*

"Well is it cheap?"

*Of course not, but it still has 2% more alcohol, so the price is 400% more.*

"That's sounds lovely. Do you have any overpriced food?"

*Only the most expensive burgers and fries. We meticulously place it on an irregular plate for photographs to share with your friends.*

"Perfect."

*Can I get you some unchilled water poured from a pirate bottle?*

"Please."

*Great — thanks for stopping by. Enjoy the eclectic music and decor.*

"Oh . . . I love this band."

*Probably not. They just formed yesterday.*

## A.I.

Magazine selfie
smudges of mirrors
reflecting self-
loathing bathroom
lines out the door with
mood ring moments
swirling in a
vintage cloudy
raging rain
beyond blurring
boundary lines.

Forecasted—
Now here!
The frightening
build of
evil present,
Once fiction,
Now the
frilling mad
reality of
a world
always coming to an
apocalyptic end.

Ignoring resilience
of the roaches
crawling over
scolding earth,
Holistically jarring

truths of a
cracking reflection,
Ok to raise
and ravage
each other's daughter.

## Cliché 'Merica

Muggy air
lingering above
contradictory
long stairs,
To the top
in left out field
where only the
bold and futile
live with the
beautiful,
Influenced
by mean
phosphorescent green
of fading promises that
someday this will all
still be around
long after the imploding
lies of emotion
of pretend
commissioning too
big to fail glazed
over read
rights that Miranda
still hasn't heard,

Sweet as sex
trafficking inc.
to make sure he has a nice
soft face to emblazon upon
warp speed space races,

Queens of the boneage left
to sing that
we are the proverbial champions of
the stadium wave.

**Black Cat**

Black cat
darting
across the street with
white and yellow eyes
glowing
from calm stares at
oncoming
onslaughts
of impeccably
timed takers,
Shrieking a
deep cry
from his bosom
cutting through
airtight
glass
as people circle
around him, Fur
tingling through
his retractable
glare,
A clicking countdown
to his ruminating end.

## Dead Babies

Silently held screams of
terror from
lips gently moving
as mini feet sway
back and forth
over a splintered floor,
Time and again
crawling
towards us with
drool dribbling
down their
insatiable gullies,
Hissing out
their spineless figures.
Gulping greedy
green riddles
of powder ashes spraying
into elongating shadows
from setting sons,
Guns to their
small tender
heads blasting
smears
of empty brain
brilliance into
a kaleidoscope
dripping into
the drain . . .

My sweet vanity
baby laying
in a mass grave.

**Night Terror**

Fire starter
of dissident
distant lands,
Churning panic
through murders
reminiscent of antiquity,
Antiquely,
Distinctly,
Greedy,
The knife
gliding into
my lovers back.

Dreams of mother
withering away . . .

**Oliver Twist**

The white choir
bellowing
as strings release wails
of echoing walls
of poor wet cobblestone
... boy.

This orphan
business is sad,
An all-over twist
of solvent
solvers
with a knack
for wasting time,

Swirling emotions
of a woman whose
light
is eternally
adept,
A voice rising
from the other
side of space,


I confess it,
There was
no sweeter sound
than the curtain
and heavenly crown.

Shh!
The look,
The hands,
and the delivery,

The world is a dream.

**People-Controlled Content**

TV flicking
dials
into one-
way messages,
Approved
for the masses by
the United
Covenant of lords
and ladies,
The Lotus whizzing by
at incredible
floating speeds,
Mired by
jaded ponds of
wincing lenses,
My squinting eyes
peaking over a
veranda.

The revolution
not televised to
a new
handheld generation,
Generating
bad Nielson
ratings
of total
demoralization,

Bravo,
to the new
twirled order.

**Pop Control**

You scum,
You lowlife
thieves,
Stealers
of position,
How dare you come
to this place
we did not create
and take what
is rightfully
not ours.

There are corners of
gentrified ghetto
streets reserved for
the law
handed down
by God-
given privileges
allowing us to dictate
rights to humans
as we see fit.

Test tubes
of might and strength,
Raped
into the pits
of earthly hell . . .
. . . The only hell...

The farce of opportunity.

**Selfie**

Hoser.
Head in the
cloudless air.
Boiling static,
An unbalancing level
with the bubble
swaying aloofly.
Clumsily unable.

**Tiptoe**

Tips of toes
at the edge
of a dingy
carpet,
A carouseling
group of mini horses
going up
and down with
faces finely
crafted of smiles
to predisposing
looks at
a little boy
circling a coffee
table at top
speeds with an
exhilarating grin,
My grandmother
clapping,
"Tippy-tippy
Toe ... tippy-
Toe ..."

**Two Lines and Freebird**

Gripping glass buzzing on my tongue,
Whistling along with God.

# PART TWO

**Love**

You capture me,
sweet maiden—
voyage across
swirling whirlpools,
Steady waves crying
my name, Choppily
pulling me back to
the surface
of sweet faint sounds,
And I'm swirling
back to you
of no force of
my own.

Silently behind
a satin
veiling smile,
A furnace burning
blunt forces of
elation colors
consuming me
as I lay there
connected
to some faint
balcony
spilling over with
treasure
pulsing under
my toes,
Ambient ponds
distantly calling

to my traipsing dreams,
Lulling me
into my
Eternity.

**Vines**

Austin city limitless
light beams,
Bouncing off of
looping grins of
lovesick helpless
hearts crashing at
time-bending speeds.

The smell
of your
wine-
stained breath
floating over
your lips,

Warm decadence
melting my inhibitions.

## Teen Mom OG

A mischievous
explorative smile,
Pressing against
a metal grating
screen falling
face forward
floating through
time screaming
terrorizing shrills
of teen mom terror.

An eternity between
the ground widening
in white eyes
of exploring
minds of
never again
misses leveling
fatherly uncertainty
of two unsure lovers
hanging on the broken
back of their
baby.

**Messiah**

Foretold Nazarene
serpent whispering,
. . . who will save us . . .
Lord,
Author of teenage dreams,
The riddler loading
his impoverish
imposing hand,
Business as usual,
The casual Messiah
warping the Petrus,
Handling
and commanding his
own chorus,
Emoting the 2nd Coming
of the sword.

## The Lotto

I saw a man
cash his lotto
ticket for $75k.
He couldn't
believe his own
eyes, Madly
pacing the
floor,
Unable to
keep his composure,
wobbling
against the
wall.

He told me
he lost his
wife 8 years ago,
And this would make
everything right.

**Changes**

Insecurity
inundated with
initiations
falling gently in
line with
the status
quotient of
nothing
spewing spun
ducktales
on the back
of Ebenezer
Stooge the 3rd
trinity
from the left
godhead,
Greed the father
the son,
and the holy
boast from eye
to eye contact
applauding our
mediocre choices.

Insecure,
Controlling,
Manipulative,
I hurt
my love
to feel less pain.

**White Girl**

Game
of phones on
fresh cut
roses burning
ashes stalling
downwardly as
dogs
face first into
blue-eyed porcelain.

A filthy mistress whispering
that she misses
her mister
and my tongue
tightening as I close
my eyes around the
idea of pure
ineffable rapture…

Silly boy,
Didn't you know?
The white lady
lies.

## Mania

Wrestling seven-
foot tall
tough guys in
tightrope
tap shoes.
Curtsies
to the crowd
roaring
to the ring
of 88 egotistical keys
pushed simultaneously to
melodies of
self-loathing.

Needy men flexing
for their reflection
in the camera lens,
saying over and over:
I am the man
of mayhem.

**Mad Men**

Pacing across
self-scrubbing
floors,
Smiles through
teeth gritting
tastings of
shrieks of
yes sirs to
make little extras
for his unfamiliar family
bidding love for his true
heart
away in some
distant land
where the wheel
keeps spinning
under the feet
of helpless souls
never knowing
another way.

**Forgot My Lines**

Pushing salty soft hair
out of King Lear's
face as he resuscitates
his old ideas of a brave
new world of
native canoes cutting
low-tide river veins,
(Meanwhile Backstage)
A young girl
crying to herself
as I approach her
placing
my hand on her
hunching shoulder,
An alarming whirl
of a strong hand striking
her face
of sheer terror
as she fervently begs for
her life . . .
(no words)

## Forever Young

Still sidewalk
cheers beneath
concrete steam,
Rising from
underneath the
taut skin of
the vernal earth,
Solar empowering
angst and voracious
victories comprised
solely of the most
original
ideas ever conceived.

A man whistled
to himself gazing from afar…

**New School**

The doctor
of funk
dancing up
street steps at
5 mph
around tight
concrete corners
with shouts of
Judah echoing off
of Daniel's lion
den dishes
dripping from
bloody fangs
ripping tears,
in my heart,
Moist lines
carving across
my cheeks;

A bow to my old friends.

# A Message from the Writer

**Final Essay**

Greetings from the other side. I wrote most of this collection in some of the most trying times of my life. I think my 20s were filled with turmoil, failure, insecurity, and exasperated victory. In no way is my experience a representation of yours. I chose to write poetry because I had a hard time expressing myself in real life. I'm still working on that.

Some people might find my poetry dark or inaccessible. I've had people ask me, "What do you mean by that line?" The truth is that poetry is like painting. You're able to see yourself in each stroke. Once I let go, the words become yours. There's no way for me to try to explain what I was feeling because I can't transport myself back to that time. The poem means what it means now to you.

My parents were teenagers when they had me, and I watched them go through their own struggles in their 20s growing up. My parents don't have college educations, and I watched how difficult it can be to raise a child with limited resources. In spite of my parents' monetary issues, they found a way to put me through private school through the 5th grade. The other gift my parents gave me was the library. The limit at the library was to check out 12 books, and I took out the maximum each time. The library was a place that there were no limits on my life. I threw myself into each book because my mind could go further than the boundaries of my surroundings.

I started writing poetry, scripts, essays, and short stories around middle school. I was an awkward and overweight kid with glasses. I was usually a troublemaker, and I settled for an identity as the class clown. I had a real issue with authoritative figures. My English projects increasingly became more creative and allowed me to express my ideas in words. I was better at that than any other thing in school. I especially loved sharing my writing with friends. My writing back then was typically edgy with a lot of things that would make my teachers cringe in their seats. Most of them let me say it. I'm eternally grateful to the ones that challenged me to be better.

This collection was the culmination of six to seven years and hundreds of poems. I've tried to select the ones I thought represented that time in my life best. I've spent countless hours trying to make them as perfect as I could, and I've frequently wanted to delete all of it on many occasions. I have four more collections planned over the next several years. Thanks for joining me. I hope you come back for the rest…

# Epilogue

**The Mirror Is Me**

Nero walking the tops
of walls listening to
to fire crackling
bones of his people as he
leers at them
with saliva
sliding down his
cheeks,
Maniacally shouting
that he's arrived
to throw everybody off
of a cliff...

Cliff...
Who are you talking to?

## Girls Are Just Boys with Makeup

Ladies with round
biceps in front of workout
ropes hanging off of
curling iron chatter
to trap the nearest
guy with all tricks
of the trade like
engaging their egos
with undivided interest.

Have you met the guy
of her dreams
comprised of
all of her fantasies
of half-witted,
at least tall,
dimwit who
can't utter a sentence
except that football
is complex beauty
as he crashes his
head into another beer
can fumbling over
the idea that there's
no homoeroticism
in MMA and
pretending that buff
girls don't look like
buff guys.

**Old Ladies Write Poetry**

Walkers rolling over stale
carpet to a microphone
to read clever word
riddles that Dawn used
to be a slightly naughty
girl with a schoolboy
from long ago.

Hot love
still stirring a cold heart
through veiny vascular
word similes
like mother's warm
apple pie sitting
on window seals
of yesteryears memories
as soft self-congratulatory
chuckles hold nobody
in suspense except Ethel,
who can't remember the
last time she went to the
bathroom.

**Rashad**

Flashing plights
moving at lightning
pace across cheaply
illuminating dance
floors under basements
with falling asbestos
onto bobbing heads
back and forth
as an artist
medicates his
moving mind
across lonely
periods in between
paint sweat swaths
of every booming element
in rich empty
clever logic eyes
to dancing
homeless feet
on bare broken
glass floors
stomping on
every insecurity
of a larger largesse,

Two empty
cups to pour
one for my friend.

**Send in the Clowns**

There we are
marred by dirt
from our
distraction camps
as I touch
a barcode over
my frail hands
holding a towel and
bar of soap to wash
white powder
into my charred skin.

Oh dear peasant,
From his grace,
A gift
to your
loving family
to hold closely
in porcelain chambers
folding over in
laughter as we
inhale cleansing air
leaking through
a shower head
losing all
sentiment and candor
to embrace
our fondest fears,

The fuhrer raising
his hands as a woman
shouts her final notes
with a crackling voice

pushing into my deep-set
eyes as I take my place
among the
court jesters
cackling to death
at everything
we never had.

## Self Portrait of a Young Artist by Not James Joyce

My masculine hands
with veins bulging as
the tap of soft keys
under each step
of my eyes blinded
by Beethoven's
opus to 88 keys
and glorious morning,
A range of sound
boxes moving across
snowcapped mountains
reaching into my soul
struggles as I gently
bang my heart on
history for a reprieve.

Please take me
to the sea on
wings of regal
seagulls gliding
air waves over
little hills
as rubble chases
behind my charging steps
toward the truth of
who I am . . .
Words breaking me
at my knees dropping
me before a savior
with hands lifted
towards the heavens.

I am lifted by my
sheer will to write
the future of the
natural earth resonating
along the time capsules
of the basic human
experience which is limitation,
A young writer
spoke to me peering
over her glasses.
You are the one,
so do whatever it
is that you can think
of because
the oceans are
moving toward the
shore swelling at
sounds of people shrills
losing their lives
crying for God to
save them as
He continues to write
the grotesque plot
of people dying senselessly
under his foot
crunching them into
the ground.
Glass in sand
mixing every grain
into a joker
jar pouring every
life into lightning
blowing waves over
sculptures of
a better world.

And I hear the
voices of my children
calling me daddy
and the soft voice
of my love calling
to them in song.

www.ingramcontent.com/pod-product-compliance
Lightning Source LLC
Chambersburg PA
CBHW061344040426
42444CB00011B/3077